FUNDAMENTALS

LAYING A FOUNDATION FOR NEW BELIEVERS

BY TOREMA THOMPSON

Hebrews 6:1-3

Therefore leaving the principles of the doctrine of Christ, let us go on unto perfection; not laying again the foundation of **repentance from dead works**, *and of* **faith toward God**, *Of the doctrine of* **baptisms**, *and of* **laying on of hands**, *and of* **resurrection of the dead**, *and of* **eternal judgment**. *And this will we do, if God permit.*

<u>CONTENTS</u>

WELCOME HOME!

Dear Treasured One,

Welcome home! You are loved, you are special, and you fit perfectly into His family; His Body; His Church. Accepting Jesus as your personal Lord and Saviour is the best decision you will ever make! Not only am I rejoicing with you, but Heaven is as well.

> *"In the same way, there is joy in the presence of God's angels when even one sinner repents."* (Luke 15:10, NLT)

You have put your trust in Jesus Christ, the Son of God; you have accepted His perfect sacrifice on the cross and have believed in your heart that God raised Him from the dead. Because of your confession of faith, your name is written in the Lamb's book of life. By the blood of Jesus, you have been made clean in the sight of the Father in Heaven, and the debt you owed for your sins has been cleared—FOREVER! You are now righteous because of Jesus; therefore, you can now come BOLDLY before the Father as His child. What a privilege!

"Everyone who acknowledges me publicly here on earth, I will also acknowledge before my Father in heaven." (Matthew 10:32, NLT)

Because of Christ and our faith in Him, we can now come boldly and confidently into God's presence. (Ephesians 3:12, NLT)

You are now a part of the household of faith (Galatians 6:10) and all things are yours. You belong to Christ and Christ belongs to God (1 Corinthians 3:21-23); you have the God of all creation on your side! What and who should you now fear? What would God not do for you or give to you when He has already given you His Son? What can you not overcome now that you are in Him?

And we know that God causes everything to work together for the good of those who love God and are called according to his purpose for them. For God knew his people in advance, and he chose them to become like his Son, so that his Son would be the firstborn among many brothers and sisters. And having chosen them, he called them to come to him. And having called them, he gave them right standing with himself. And having given them right standing, he gave them his glory.

What shall we say about such wonderful things as these? If God is for us, who can ever be against us? Since he did not spare even his own Son but gave him up for us all, won't he also give us everything else? Who dares accuse us whom God has chosen for his own? No one— for God himself has given us right standing with himself. Who then will condemn us? No one— for Christ Jesus died for us and was raised to life for us, and he is sitting in the place of honor at God's right hand, pleading for us.

Can anything ever separate us from Christ's love? Does it mean he no longer loves us if we have trouble or calamity, or are persecuted, or hungry, or destitute, or in danger, or threatened with death? (As the Scriptures say, "For your sake we are killed every day; we are being slaughtered like sheep.") No, despite all these things, overwhelming victory is ours through Christ, who loved us.

And I am convinced that nothing can ever separate us from God's love. Neither death nor life, neither angels nor demons, neither our fears for today nor our worries about tomorrow—not even the powers of hell can separate us from God's love. No power in the sky above or in the earth below—indeed, nothing in all creation will ever be able to separate us from the love of

God that is revealed in Christ Jesus our Lord. (Romans 8:28-39, NLT)

INTRODUCTION

The purpose of this book is to lay out those teachings considered to be foundational to every believer's walk in Christ. If you are to move on towards maturity in Christ, as God desires, it is crucial that you know, understand and believe these principles.

> *Therefore leaving the principles of the doctrine of Christ, let us go on unto perfection; not laying again the foundation of <u>repentance from dead works</u>, and of <u>faith toward God</u>, Of the doctrine of <u>baptisms</u>, and of <u>laying on of hands</u>, and of <u>resurrection of the dead</u>, and of <u>eternal judgment</u>. And this will we do, if God permit. (Hebrews 6:1-3, emphasis mine)*

In the following pages, you will find one chapter devoted to each of the ideals that have been underlined in the passage above (with baptisms divided over three chapters). The scripture above makes it clear that these topics need to be *believed, received* and *applied*, so that you might move on to maturity in Christ. These foundational principles should form a springboard into your maturation process, not become a resting place.

Scripture tells us that you are God's building (1 Corinthians 3:9). In the natural, the height of a building is limited to the depth of its foundation; similarly, if you are to grow to the height the Lord intended, then the foundation of your Christian life must firstly reach the depth that He desires it to. If we cut corners at this stage, although the hindrances may only appear to be small to begin with, as you move on further in your walk with the Lord, these hindrances will only become greater, stunting your growth. In other words, if the correct foundation is not laid at the onset, you could end up living a life way below the standard that God has for you.

So, as you read through this book *(as many times as you need to)*, pray that the correct foundation will be laid for your life. As you discover the foundational principles and elementary teachings of Christ, be willing to believe, receive *and apply* what you learn, so that, ultimately, you might move on to perfection (spiritual maturity) as the Lord desires.

CHAPTER 1:

REPENTANCE FROM DEAD WORKS

REPENTANCE

Repent. That's not a word we hear very often these days, is it? However, after Peter (one of Jesus' twelve apostles) stood up to preach on the day of Pentecost, that was the first instruction he gave to the Jews when they asked him what they should do to be saved.

> *Now when they heard this, they were pricked in their heart, and said unto Peter and to the rest of the apostles, Men and brethren, what shall we do? Then Peter said unto them, Repent, and be baptized every one of you in the name of Jesus Christ for the remission of sins, and ye shall receive the gift of the Holy Ghost. For the promise is unto you, and to your children, and to all that are afar off, even as many as the Lord our God shall call. (Acts 2:37-39, emphasis mine)*

Repentance is an absolute prerequisite for true salvation. It is not simply to say you are 'sorry' but is a grief, pain and remorse that comes from the heart, leading to a change in the direction and course of your life.

> *Prove by the way you live that you have repented of your sins and turned to God...*
> *(Luke 3:8a NLT)*

To repent speaks of a turning; one that begins as a decision in your heart and becomes manifested in your speech and actions.

> *For the kind of sorrow God wants us to experience leads us away from sin and results in salvation. There's no regret for that kind of sorrow. But worldly sorrow, which lacks repentance, results in spiritual death.*
> *(2 Corinthians 7:10, NLT)*

Godly sorrow doesn't just leave us feeling bad about ourselves but causes us to identify that our thoughts, motives and actions have been contrary to God. True repentance causes us to turn away from the sin that we loved before and towards *He* that is good. Worldly sorrow, on the other hand, may leave a person recognising that they have done wrong, but it carries no regret and no acknowledgement of the need for salvation. Rather than causing a person to turn from sin, it causes a person to experience condemnation, self-justification or pride, all things that cause a person to remain in their sinful state rather than be freed from it. As the scripture above reveals, we can identify worldly sorrow because it lacks repentance (a turning). The only result in a failure to turn from sin is to fall deeper and deeper into its grips and further into darkness and spiritual death.

> Don't you realize that you become the slave of whatever you choose to obey? You can be a slave to sin, which leads to death, or you can choose to obey God, which leads to righteous living. Thank God! Once you were slaves of sin, but now you wholeheartedly obey this teaching we have given you. (Romans 6:16-17, NLT)

True repentance causes us to obey the call of the Gospel, by turning from one slave master (sin) to the True Master, Jesus Christ, Who is able to save and give the power to live free from sin.

FROM DEAD WORKS

> Don't you realize that those who do wrong will not inherit the Kingdom of God? Don't fool yourselves. Those who indulge in sexual sin, or

who worship idols, or commit adultery, or are male prostitutes, or practice homosexuality, or are thieves, or greedy people, or drunkards, or are abusive, or cheat people—none of these will inherit the Kingdom of God. Some of you were once like that. But you were cleansed; you were made holy; you were made right with God by calling on the name of the Lord Jesus Christ and by the Spirit of our God.
(1 Corinthians 6:9-11, NLT)

Now the works of the flesh are manifest, which are these; Adultery, fornication, uncleanness, lasciviousness, Idolatry, witchcraft, hatred, variance, emulations, wrath, strife, seditions, heresies, Envyings, murders, drunkenness, revellings, and such like: of the which I tell you before, as I have also told you in time past, that they which do such things shall not inherit the kingdom of God. (Galatians 5:19-21)

Dead works are anything that come from the flesh; that is anything done through our sinful / carnal nature, anything done outside of God's will and order. When a person repents, this is what they are making a decision to turn from. Most of us grow up believing that we are "good", "not as bad as so and so" or that we can somehow be good outside of God, but this is a lie! Less commonly, there are some people who consider *themselves* to be "a nasty piece of work" or in other words, not a nice person; however, even then there is a kind of pride or acceptance in this that says, "this is just the way I am, don't try to change me!" Regardless, of which end of the spectrum a person finds themselves to be, outside of Christ Jesus, every human being falls short of the glorious standard of God; it is of this self-sufficiency and this self-autonomy for which repentance is required.

> *For all have sinned, and come short of the glory of God; (Romans 3:23)*

Irrespective of the specifics of a person's sin, outside of Christ, all their works are worthless. No matter how many good things a person tries to do or say, or how many religious prayers or sacrifices they may offer up, outside of Christ Jesus everything is in vain. Outside of Christ, it is all filthy rags.

> *We are all infected and impure with sin. When we display our righteous deeds, they are nothing but filthy rags. Like autumn leaves, we wither and fall, and our sins sweep us away like the wind. (Isaiah 64:6, NLT)*

ACCEPTING CHRIST WITHOUT REPENTANCE?

Now, there is a common practice that has arisen within the church, where unbelievers are given the opportunity to accept Jesus without firstly repenting of their sin. We will look at "faith towards God" and receiving the gift of salvation in the next chapter; however, let's just touch on this concept briefly.

Sin and Christ are at opposing ends; hence, if Jesus is standing at North (with salvation), but a person is facing South towards sin, it is categorically *impossible* for them to receive the gift of Christ whilst their back is towards Him.

> *For to be carnally minded is death; but to be spiritually minded is life and peace. Because the carnal mind is enmity against God: for it is not subject to the law of God, neither indeed can be. So then they that are in the flesh cannot please God. (Romans 8:6-8)*

As we have discussed throughout this chapter, repentance is essentially a 180-degree turnaround. Before a person can receive Jesus, they must turn so that they are facing His direction. The only reason a person would turn in

the first place, is if they have believed the bad
news (which is that they are sinners separated
from God and living a life contrary to His will),
and secondly, if they have believed the Good
News (which is that God desires to be reconciled
to them and has made a way for that to be
possible through Jesus). Only at the point of true
belief would a person repent (turn) so that they
can receive Jesus. If a person claims to believe
but does not repent, then according to
Scripture, they do not believe. Likewise, if a
person claims to have received Jesus but has
never repented (turned from their sin), then
again, according to Scripture, they are not
saved.

*Bring forth fruit that is consistent with
repentance [let your lives prove your change
of heart]; (Matthew 3:8, AMPC)*

Now, we know that repentance doesn't mean
that you will not be tempted with certain sins
ever again; however, there is a difference
between a temptation, and living in habitual sin
i.e. deciding to pursue sin, condone sin or remain
in it.

*We know that God's children do not make a
practice of sinning, for God's Son holds them*

> *securely, and the evil one cannot touch*
> *them. (1 John 5:18, NLT)*

A person who pursues sin, accepts sin as right, loves sin and continues in sin, whilst claiming to have received Jesus is a liar. If they really do believe that they have received Jesus but have not repented from their sin, the sad truth is that they have received a counterfeit Jesus—the devil disguise!

> *And it is no wonder, for Satan himself*
> *masquerades as an angel of light; (2*
> *Corinthians 11:14, AMPC)*

> *Anyone who continues to live in him will not*
> *sin. But anyone who keeps on sinning does not*
> *know him or understand who he is. Dear*
> *children, don't let anyone deceive you about*
> *this: When people do what is right, it shows*
> *that they are righteous, even as Christ is*
> *righteous. But when people keep on sinning, it*
> *shows that they belong to the devil, who has*
> *been sinning since the beginning. But the Son*
> *of God came to destroy the works of the devil.*
> *(1 John 3:6-8, NLT)*

God's kindness is never to leave or encourage a person to remain in their sin, because sin is bondage! Jesus died to free us from sin and to restore us to a right standing relationship with the Father. Any so-called "gospel" message that encourages a person to *remain* as they are and to simply add Jesus as an addition to their life is not the true Gospel and carries no power.

> *Don't you see how wonderfully kind, tolerant, and patient God is with you? Does this mean nothing to you? Can't you see that his kindness is intended to turn you from your sin? (Romans 2:4, NLT)*

So, as we can see, God is kind, but His kindness is intended to cause us to repent *from* dead works, not remain in them. In the next chapter, we will discuss what repentance from dead works brings us *towards*.

CHAPTER 2:

FAITH TOWARDS GOD

I have had one message for Jews and Greeks alike—the necessity of repenting from sin and turning to God, and of having faith in our Lord Jesus. (Acts 20:21, NLT)

In the kingdom of God, there is a "leave to cleave" principle at work. Simply put, we are always required to firstly *leave* something in order to *cleave* to something else.

Therefore shall a man leave his father and his mother, and shall cleave unto his wife: and they shall be one flesh. (Genesis 2:24)

In the same way that a man is required to leave his mother and father in order to cleave to his wife, we are also required to leave behind this world in order to cleave to God. This is how we demonstrate our faith; this is how we demonstrate our trust in God. God will not give us the new unless we are firstly willing to let go of the old.

If we apply this principle to what we have discussed so far in this book, you will recognise that repentance is the "leaving" part of this principle. Before a person can "cleave" to God, receiving righteousness and salvation, they must firstly choose to turn from sin. It is in this turn of faith of the heart (leaving) that the Lord faithfully steps in, and thus a cleaving can take place. When an individual makes the decision in their heart to repent, they are turning from dead works and trusting (by faith) that God is faithful to save them as they turn to Him.

> *That if thou shalt confess with thy mouth the Lord Jesus, and shalt believe in thine heart that God hath raised him from the dead, thou shalt be saved. For with the heart man believeth unto righteousness; and with the mouth confession is made unto salvation. For the scripture saith, Whosoever believeth on him shall not be ashamed. (Romans 10:9-11)*

When a person repents, they are actively putting their faith in God (Who they cannot see) to make Himself personal and present as He has promised. Through this act of faith they are saying that they know they cannot make themselves righteous but are trusting in the power of God through Christ Jesus. When a person repents, they are saying they know they would never be able to meet God's standard of righteousness but are choosing to believe that if they put their faith in Jesus, God *will* forgive their sins and make them right in His sight.

> *We are made right with God by placing our faith in Jesus Christ. And this is true for everyone who believes, no matter who we are. (Romans 3:22, NLT)*

GRACE NOT WORKS

> *God saved you by his grace when you believed. And you can't take credit for this; it is a gift from God. Salvation is not a reward for the good things we have done, so none of us can boast about it. (Ephesians 2:8-9, NLT)*

Now, in the previous chapter we identified that true repentance would lead to a turning away from sin. This is not to be misconstrued with "getting it all together" or "making yourself right" and *then* coming to God (this is impossible anyway). Although people can only identify true repentance as time goes by (through the fruits of a person's life), God on the other hand, sees the heart of man and He is able to identify, at the very moment a person believes and confesses, whether their heart is genuine or not. For everyone who truly does believe that turning from sin and in faith *towards* Jesus will save them, God knows, and immediately saves their soul by taking them out of the enemy's camp of darkness and placing them into the Kingdom of Light.

> *[The Father] has delivered and drawn us to Himself out of the control and the dominion of darkness and has transferred us into the kingdom of the Son of His love,*
> *(Colossians 1:13, AMPC)*

Repentance of the heart is a decision of faith because the reality is, not one person is able to truly turn from sin without the grace (empowerment) of God anyway. When a person repents in their heart, they are *simultaneously* putting their faith in Jesus to make them new and to give them the ability to live free from sin - just like He did.

> *Therefore if any man be in Christ, he is a new creature: old things are passed away; behold, all things are become new.*
> *(2 Corinthians 5:17)*

But to as many as did receive and welcome Him, He gave the authority (power, privilege, right) to become the children of God, that is, to those who believe in (adhere to, trust in, and rely on) His name— (John 1:12, AMPC)

So you see, a person does not start living righteously in order for God to save them. No, righteousness and a transformed life are the *RESULT* of true salvation. At the moment a person puts their trust in Jesus, they become a new creation, born of God, now able to desire and do what God desires.

When you were slaves to sin, you were free from the obligation to do right. And what was the result? You are now ashamed of the things you used to do, things that end in eternal doom. But now you are free from the power of sin and have become slaves of God. Now you do those things that lead to holiness and result in eternal life. For the wages of sin is death, but the free gift of God is eternal life through Christ Jesus our Lord. (Romans 6:20-23, NLT)

Before we received salvation, we were all slaves to sin and could not live righteously even if we tried. However, when we turned to Christ, by faith, we received a new heart and a new spirit

(His Spirit) which means we now have new desires and a new ability to do the things that please the Father, just like Jesus demonstrated when He was on the earth (John 8:29).

> *A new heart also will I give you, and a new spirit will I put within you: and I will take away the stony heart out of your flesh, and I will give you an heart of flesh. (Ezekiel 36:26)*

WHAT'S IN THE GIFT?

As you can see, salvation is the wonderful gift of God received the very moment we turned from our sin and trusted in Christ Jesus our Lord. But what does this gift contain? Let's briefly discuss what we received through salvation.

- OUR DEBT WAS CLEARED

Sin had a penalty and that penalty was death—eternal death (separation from God, the Source of all life). When we received the gift of salvation our debt was cleared completely. *Hallelujah!*

> *For the wages of sin is death; but the gift of God is eternal life through Jesus Christ our Lord. (Romans 6:23)*

*He has removed our sins as far from us as the
east is from the west. (Psalm 103:12, NLT)*

- WE RECEIVED RIGHTEOUSNESS

Not only was our penalty paid, but we were also
made righteous, holy, clean and pure before
God. We could never work to receive this; it was
given to us as a gift. Where sin used to keep us
from His presence, we can now enjoy a *personal*
and *intimate* relationship with Him.

> *Therefore being justified by faith, we have
> peace with God through our Lord Jesus Christ:
> (Romans 5:1)*

> *And so, dear brothers and sisters, we can
> boldly enter heaven's Most Holy Place
> because of the blood of Jesus. By his death,
> Jesus opened a new and life-giving way
> through the curtain into the Most Holy Place.
> (Hebrews 10:19-20, NLT)*

- WE BECAME ONE SPIRIT WITH CHRIST

At the moment we accepted Christ Jesus, our
spirit became one with His Spirit (or we could say
that He engulfed us into Himself); essentially, we

no longer exist - only Christ. Everything He is, we are too. His Spirit *is* our spirit.

> *But the person who is united to the Lord becomes one spirit with Him.*
> *(1 Corinthians 6:17, AMPC)*
>
> *For ye are dead, and your life is hid with Christ in God. (Colossians 3:3)*
>
> *For in Christ Jesus you are all sons of God through faith. For as many [of you] as were baptized into Christ [into a spiritual union and communion with Christ, the Anointed One, the Messiah] have put on (clothed yourselves with) Christ. (Galatians 3:26-27, AMPC)*

- WE WERE ADOPTED

We used to be orphans, estranged from our Heavenly Father. But through our union with Jesus, we became children of God, born into the eternal family.

> *So you have not received a spirit that makes you fearful slaves. Instead, you received God's Spirit when he adopted you as his own children. Now we call him, "Abba, Father." For his Spirit joins with our spirit to affirm that we are God's children. (Romans 8:15-16, NLT)*

- WE BECAME HEIRS WITH CHRIST

We are no longer just your average Jo Bloggs. Our inheritance has changed, our nature has changed... through Jesus we are royalty!

> *And if children, then heirs; heirs of God, and joint-heirs with Christ; if so be that we suffer with him, that we may be also glorified together. (Romans 8:17)*

> *But God is so rich in mercy, and he loved us so much, that even though we were dead because of our sins, he gave us life when he raised Christ from the dead. (It is only by God's grace that you have been saved!) For he raised us from the dead along with Christ and seated us with him in the heavenly realms because we are united with Christ Jesus. So God can point to us in all future ages as examples of the incredible wealth of his grace and kindness toward us, as shown in all he has done for us who are united with Christ Jesus. (Ephesians 2:4-7, NLT)*

- WE RECEIVED PROMISES OF GLORY

We have the promise of eternal life, yet the Body we have now is dying. When we were saved, we received promises of a new body and a new home; a body that will never die and a home that will never see corruption. This earth is not our home, we are simply sojourners.

We were given this hope when we were saved. (If we already have something, we don't need to hope for it. But if we look forward to something we don't yet have, we must wait patiently and confidently.) (Romans 8:24-25, NLT)

In my Father's house are many mansions: if it were not so, I would have told you. I go to prepare a place for you. And if I go and prepare a place for you, I will come again, and receive you unto myself; that where I am, there ye may be also. (John 14:2-3)

But let me reveal to you a wonderful secret. We will not all die, but we will all be transformed! It will happen in a moment, in the blink of an eye, when the last trumpet is blown. For when the trumpet sounds, those who have died will be raised to live forever. And we who are living will also be transformed. For our dying bodies must be transformed into bodies that will never die; our mortal bodies must be transformed into immortal bodies. (1 Corinthians 15:51-53, NLT)

- WE BECAME ELIGIBLE TO FULFIL OUR
  PURPOSE

We used to have our own plan for life, but God
saved us so that we could do what He planned
for us to do all along. When we were saved, we
became eligible to actually say "yes" to God's
plan and begin the process of learning
obedience.

> *For we are God's masterpiece. He has
> created us anew in Christ Jesus, so we can do
> the good things he planned for us long ago.
> (Ephesians 2:10, NLT)*

- WE RECEIVED HEALING POWER

When we were saved, we remained in this fallen
world and this fallen body; however, we were
given the power to overcome every pain,
sickness and disease both internally and
externally; emotionally and physically.

> *He personally bore our sins in His [own] body
> on the tree [as on an altar and offered Himself
> on it], that we might die (cease to exist) to sin
> and live to righteousness. By His wounds you
> have been healed. (1 Peter 2:24, AMPC)*

What a miraculous gift salvation is; truly it is a divine exchange! The remainder of your life in Christ will be an adventurous journey of unpacking these truths and experiencing the full manifestation of them in your life.

FAITH IN THE SON

When a person turns from dead works and in faith towards God, they have to trust in the salvation available through Jesus (the Messiah / Christ / Anointed One). In this section, we will summarise the key factors that validate why He is the only One we could put our trust in for salvation.

> *Let not your heart be troubled: ye believe in God, believe also in me. (John 14:1)*

Many people have no issue with believing in "God". They can acknowledge the existence of someone who is sovereign, all powerful, eternal, omnipresent and unseen; however, when it comes to the idea that God has a Son and the need for the sacrifice of the cross—this is where the rubber hits the road. Yet, this is the very way God chose to bring salvation to mankind.

For the preaching of the cross is to them that perish foolishness; but unto us which are saved it is the power of God. (1 Corinthians 1:18)

But we preach Christ crucified, unto the Jews a stumblingblock, and unto the Greeks foolishness; (1 Corinthians 1:23)

If a person claims to believe in God, but refuses to acknowledge His Son, then the God that they claim to believe in, is not the God of Heaven. Jesus is the One that revealed the Father to us in bodily form. Without the manifestation of the Son in the earth, we would never truly know the nature of the Father, neither would we be able to be reconciled to Him.

For God so loved the world, that he gave his only begotten Son, that whosoever believeth in him should not perish, but have everlasting life. (John 3:16)

Anyone who denies the Son doesn't have the Father, either. But anyone who acknowledges the Son has the Father also. (1 John 2:23, NLT)

No man has ever seen God at any time; the only unique Son, or the only begotten God, Who is in the bosom [in the intimate presence] of the Father, He has declared Him [He has

> *revealed Him and brought Him out where He can be seen; He has interpreted Him and He has made Him known]. (John 1:18, AMPC)*

THE NEED FOR A SACRIFCE

Before we confirm why Jesus is our best and ONLY option for a sacrifice, let's quickly outline why a sacrifice was even needed.

Anyone can recognise that mankind has a problem—that problem is sin. Since the first man in history fell (Adam), every person born into this world since then is plagued by the same fatal defect.

> *Therefore, as sin came into the world through one man, and death as the result of sin, so death spread to all men, [no one being able to stop it or to escape its power] because all men sinned. (Romans 5:12, AMPC)*

In short, sin is breaking God's commandments. Because God is holy, righteous and good, everything He institutes is also holy, righteous and good; therefore, a lack of adherence to His laws is innately evil. Sin separates us from God because God is the Source of all life, all light and all goodness; therefore, separated from Him the only tendency of man is to fall towards darkness, depravity *and death*.

> *But your iniquities have made a separation between you and your God, and your sins have hidden His face from you, so that He will not hear. (Isaiah 59:2, AMPC)*

Now, according to the law of Moses (the old covenant of God), the only way a person could be purified and forgiven was for blood to be shed.

> *In fact, according to the law of Moses, nearly everything was purified with blood. For without the shedding of blood, there is no forgiveness. (Hebrews 9:22, NLT)*

The blood of a thing contains its life. As we saw previously, the penalty for sin is death (Romans 6:23); therefore, in order for a person not to die for their own sin, another life (sacrifice) is required in their place.

> *for the life of the body is in its blood. I have given you the blood on the altar to purify you, making you right with the Lord. It is the blood,*

> *given in exchange for a life, that makes*
> *purification possible. (Leviticus 17:11, NLT)*

Under the old covenant, there were a vast number of rules, regulations and instructions about how sacrifices were to be made, on what days they were to be made, what animals should be sacrificed for different sins and the list goes on! The thing with all these sacrifices, was that the life of animals was never enough to completely take away a person's sin. Hence, these sacrifices had to be performed over and over again, year after year after year!

> *The old system under the law of Moses was only a shadow, a dim preview of the good things to come, not the good things themselves. The sacrifices under that system were repeated again and again, year after year, but they were never able to provide perfect cleansing for those who came to worship. If they could have provided perfect cleansing, the sacrifices would have stopped, for the worshipers would have been purified once for all time, and their feelings of guilt would have disappeared. But instead, those sacrifices actually reminded them of their sins year after year. For it is not possible for the blood of bulls and goats to take away sins. That is why, when Christ came into the world,*

he said to God, "You did not want animal sacrifices or sin offerings. But you have given me a body to offer. You were not pleased with burnt offerings or other offerings for sin. Then I said, 'Look, I have come to do your will, O God— as is written about me in the Scriptures.'" First, Christ said, "You did not want animal sacrifices or sin offerings or burnt offerings or other offerings for sin, nor were you pleased with them" (though they are required by the law of Moses). Then he said, "Look, I have come to do your will." He cancels the first covenant in order to put the second into effect. For God's will was for us to be made holy by the sacrifice of the body of Jesus Christ, <u>once for all time</u>. (Hebrews 10:1-4, NLT, emphasis mine)

Enter Jesus, the Saviour of the whole world (John 1:29). Since we have all sinned, we ALL require a sacrifice. There is none among men that could save us, so God Himself came down to Earth to become the sacrifice for us. Wow, what love!

When we were utterly helpless, Christ came at just the right time and died for us sinners. Now, most people would not be willing to die for an upright person, though someone might perhaps be willing to die for a person who is especially good. But God showed his great

> *love for us by sending Christ to die for us while*
> *we were still sinners. (Romans 5:6-8, NLT)*

It was never His desire for animal sacrifices to take away our sins; He knew from before the foundation of the world, what He would do and that was to send His one and only Son, Jesus (Revelation 13:8).

> *Jesus said to him, I am the Way and the Truth*
> *and the Life; no one comes to the Father*
> *except by (through) Me. (John 14:16, AMPC)*

Let's finally look at some of the key factors as to why we can put our trust in Jesus, the one and ONLY worthy sacrifice for our sins, and the one and ONLY way to the Father in Heaven.

- JESUS IS GOD

> *In the beginning was the Word, and the Word*
> *was with God, and the Word was God. The*
> *same was in the beginning with God. All things*
> *were made by him; and without him was not*
> *any thing made that was made. In him was*
> *life; and the life was the light of men.*
> *(John 1:1-4)*

And the Word was made flesh, and dwelt among us, (and we beheld his glory, the glory as of the only begotten of the Father,) full of grace and truth. (John 1:14)

Before Jesus came to earth as a man, He was the Word in Heaven. He always existed with the Father and through Him was everything created.

Jesus said unto them, Verily, verily, I say unto you, Before Abraham was, I am. (John 5:58)

Christ is the visible image of the invisible God. He existed before anything was created and is supreme over all creation, (Colossians 1:15, NLT)

One of the reasons the Jewish leaders hated Jesus when He was on the earth, was because He proclaimed that God was His Father. In declaring Himself to be the Son of God, Jesus was revealing the Godhead in a way humanity did not yet know them.

But Jesus replied, "My Father is always working, and so am I." So the Jewish leaders tried all the harder to find a way to kill him. For he not only broke the Sabbath, he called God his Father, thereby making himself equal with God. (John 5:17-18, NLT)

Jesus had to be God in order for His sacrifice to be worth the sins of all mankind. Nevertheless, He also had to become man in order that He might die and shed His life (blood) on behalf of all humanity. If He was *just* a man with the same blood as Adam (like everybody else), He would have needed a saviour also. However, the fact that He was God and was conceived into the world supernaturally, made Him the perfect candidate.

- JESUS WAS CONCEIVED SUPERNATURALLY

Therefore the Lord himself shall give you a sign; Behold, a virgin shall conceive, and bear a son, and shall call his name Immanuel. (Isaiah 7:14)

Biblically, the lineage of man could be traced through the male line all the way back to Adam. As we look through this line, every person in history fell short of the glory of God; everyone sinned, everyone died, and everyone needed a saviour.

For as in Adam all die, even so in Christ shall all be made alive. (1 Corinthians 15:22)

Therefore, in order for Jesus to redeem the world, He needed a different type of heritage; He needed supernatural blood. Through the supernatural conception, the divinity of God was encased by the frailty of humanity; thus, Jesus was legally able to enter into the world as a man (with all the rights that God gave to human beings on the earth), whilst simultaneously carrying the supernatural life (blood) of God.

> *And I will put enmity between thee and the woman, and between thy seed and her seed; it shall bruise thy head, and thou shalt bruise his heel. (Genesis 3:15)*

> *For although the first woman came from man, every other man was born from a woman, and everything comes from God.*
> *(1 Corinthians 11:12, NLT)*

- JESUS LIVED IN A BODY

> *Because God's children are human beings— made of flesh and blood—the Son also became flesh and blood. For only as a human being could he die, and only by dying could he break the power of the devil, who had the power of death (Hebrews 2:14)*

In order to die, Jesus needed a human body made of flesh and blood. How could He conquer (overcome) sin if He did not experience the same temptations as man? How could He pay the penalty for sin and defeat the power of the enemy if He was unable to die?

> *The law of Moses was unable to save us because of the weakness of our sinful nature. So God did what the law could not do. He sent his own Son in a body like the bodies we sinners have. And in that body God declared an end to sin's control over us by giving his Son as a sacrifice for our sins. (Romans 8:3, NLT)*

- JESUS LIVED WITHOUT SIN

Jesus, both God and man, lived in a human body just as we do. A body that was subjected to death because of the nature of sin that permeates the flesh. Yet, where the rest of us failed, Jesus succeeded. Hallelujah! Where the rest of us could not live according to the law of God, Jesus fulfilled it perfectly.

> *This High Priest of ours understands our weaknesses, for he faced all of the same*

testings we do, yet he did not sin. (Hebrews 4:15, NLT)

Think not that I am come to destroy the law, or the prophets: I am not come to destroy, but to fulfil. (Matthew 5:17)

- JESUS DIED ON A CROSS

But Christ has rescued us from the curse pronounced by the law. When he was hung on the cross, he took upon himself the curse for our wrongdoing. For it is written in the Scriptures, "Cursed is everyone who is hung on a tree." (Galatians 3:13, NLT)

At the appointed time in history, Jesus became our Passover Lamb (1 Corinthians 5:7). The animal sacrifices that the Jews made year after year, were only foreshadows of what the coming Messiah would do. Where the sacrifices of animals were not enough to purify man from sin, Jesus became the ultimate sacrifice once and for all.

Just think how much more the blood of Christ will purify our consciences from sinful deeds so that we can worship the living God. For by the power of the eternal Spirit, Christ offered himself to God as a perfect sacrifice for our sins. That is why he is the one who mediates a new covenant between God and people, so that all who are called can receive the eternal inheritance God has promised them. For Christ died to set them free from the penalty of the sins they had committed under that first covenant. (Hebrews 9:14-15, NLT)

- JESUS ROSE FROM THE DEAD

And that he was buried, and that he rose again the third day according to the scriptures: (1 Corinthians 15:4)

He, foreseeing this, spoke [by foreknowledge] of the resurrection of the Christ (the Messiah) that He was not deserted [in death] and left in Hades (the state of departed spirits), nor did His body know decay or see destruction. This Jesus God raised up, and of that all we [His disciples] are witnesses. (Acts 2:31-32, AMPC)

Jesus was sinless; therefore, it was impossible for death to hold Him down. The resurrection of Christ proves that He is indeed the Son of God, the Saviour of the whole world! If He had been a sinner as the rest of us were, then He would still be in the grave today. If He were not raised from the dead, then we would still be in our sins; but by the grace of God, we are free forevermore!

And if Christ be not risen, then is our preaching vain, and your faith is also vain... And if Christ be not raised, your faith is vain; ye are yet in your sins. (1 Corinthians 15:14, 17)

But the fact is that Christ (the Messiah) has been raised from the dead, and He became the firstfruits of those who have fallen asleep [in death]. (1 Corinthians 15:20, AMPC)

So you see, when we turn in faith towards God, we can be *confident* that our faith is in *He* that has the power to save us from our sin—*Jesus*, the name above every other name!

Neither is there salvation in any other: for there is none other name under heaven given among men, whereby we must be saved. (Acts 4:12)

Wherefore God also hath highly exalted him, and given him a name which is above every name: That at the name of Jesus every knee should bow, of things in heaven, and things in earth, and things under the earth; And that every tongue should confess that Jesus Christ is Lord, to the glory of God the Father. (Philippians 2:9-11)

CHAPTER 3:

BAPTISM INTO (THE BODY OF) CHRIST

Baptism is a word that means immersion or submersion. In this chapter, we will look at the baptism that takes place at the point of salvation. We have already touched on this in the previous chapter; however, we will magnify in on it a little more here.

> *For by one Spirit are we all baptized into one body, whether we be Jews or Gentiles, whether we be bond or free; and have been all made to drink into one Spirit.*
> *(1 Corinthians 12:13)*

The Body of Christ is a literal, but spiritual, vessel that houses every believer in Jesus Christ. In fact, the story of Noah and the ark that he built to save his family and two of every kind of animal from the flood, is a depiction or foreshadow of salvation through Christ (see Genesis chapters 6 to 9 for the full story). When God sent the flood to wipe away mankind from off the earth, the only way a person could be saved (rescued) from God's wrath, was to get inside the ark that God commanded Noah to build. Unfortunately, there were only eight people that survived God's wrath at that time: Noah, his wife, his three sons and their three wives.

> *And He spared not the ancient world, but preserved Noah, a preacher of righteousness, with seven other persons, when He brought a flood upon the world of ungodly [people]. (2 Peter 2:5, AMPC)*

Today, the only way to survive the wrath of God, is to believe in His Son, Jesus Christ, whom He sent.

> *And he who believes in (has faith in, clings to, relies on) the Son has (now possesses) eternal life. But whoever disobeys (is unbelieving toward, refuses to trust in, disregards, is not subject to) the Son will never see (experience) life, but [instead] the wrath of God abides on him. [God's displeasure remains on him; His indignation hangs over him continually.] (John 3:36, AMPC)*

Jesus is our Ark. When we put our faith in Jesus we were immediately taken out of the world (darkness) and placed (literally) into His Kingdom of Light. When we believed in Jesus, we were immediately saved from God's wrath and freed from all condemnation. When we put our faith in Jesus we were *immersed* or *submerged* into His spiritual Body where there is protection and liberty from the enemy's grips.

> *For as many [of you] as were baptized into Christ [into a spiritual union and communion with Christ, the Anointed One, the Messiah] have put on (clothed yourselves with) Christ. (Galatians 3:27, AMPC)*

> *...for God's Son holds them securely, and the evil one cannot touch them. (1 John 5:18b)*

This is why scripture says we are "in" Christ, because quite literally we are *in* Him. Our spirits have been clothed by His Spirit. Our spirits are now one. What He is, we now are.

> *Therefore if any man be <u>in</u> Christ, he is a new creature: old things are passed away; behold, all things are become new. (2 Corinthians 5:17, emphasis mine)*

In the Body of Christ, we each have a specific place, function or role, just as with a physical body. When we were saved, we were placed into our position in the Body and it is from this place that we are supposed to operate.

The human body has many parts, but the many parts make up one whole body. So it is with the body of Christ. Some of us are Jews, some are Gentiles, some are slaves, and some are free. But we have all been baptized into one body by one Spirit, and we all share the same Spirit. (1 Corinthians 12:12-13, NLT)

Baptism into the Body of Christ is something that took place spiritually at the very moment you believed. This was not visible to the onlooker; however, as you were baptised into Christ, *your spirit* became one with *His Spirit*. It is His Spirit that testifies with your spirit that you are now a child of God.

For his Spirit joins with our spirit to affirm that we are God's children. (Romans 8:16, NLT)

At salvation, the veil that once blinded us from the truth is removed, and everything Jesus is, we now possess in our spirit. Our spirit is perfect, just like Jesus, but it is our soul (mind, will and emotions) that is being renewed (glorified) day by day.

We are not like Moses, who put a veil over his face so the people of Israel would not see the glory, even though it was destined to fade

*away. But the people's minds were hardened, and to this day whenever the old covenant is being read, the same veil covers their minds so they cannot understand the truth. And this veil can be removed only by believing in Christ. Yes, even today when they read Moses' writings, their hearts are covered with that veil, and they do not understand. But whenever someone turns to the Lord, the veil is taken away. For the Lord is the Spirit, and wherever the Spirit of the Lord is, there is freedom. So all of us who have had that veil removed can see and reflect the glory of the Lord. And the Lord—who is the Spirit—makes us more and more like him as we are changed into his glorious image.
(2 Corinthians 3:13-18, NLT)*

Baptism into the Body of Christ is our *inward* sign of faith. However, in the next chapter we will look at baptism in water – an *outward* sign of faith.

CHAPTER 4:

BAPTISM IN WATER

As we discussed in the previous chapter, a spiritual submersion takes place at the point of salvation. The Lord identifies those who truly believe by placing them into His Body in the spirit realm. Nevertheless, although the Body of Christ (the Church) is a spiritual organism, we relate to one another in a physical environment (i.e. the *visible* realm). What this means is that even though an individual may have an *inward sign* of faith, it is their public confession of faith, through water baptism, that acts as an *outward sign* to the rest of the Body.

> *Can any man forbid water, that these should not be baptized, which have received the Holy Ghost as well as we? And he commanded them to be baptized in the name of the Lord. Then prayed they him to tarry certain days. (Acts 10:47-48)*

The context for the scripture above, is that the first Gentiles (non-Jewish people) had just received the Holy Ghost, which revealed for the first time that salvation wasn't only for the Jews, but that God desired to save the Gentiles too. In this verse, Peter, an apostle and leader in the early church, is asking a rhetorical question. He is basically saying that *they* (the Jewish believers) had no right to refuse baptism to the Gentiles since God had already identified and accepted their faith. The fact that the water baptism of the Gentiles was still something to be considered, even though they were already publicly accepted by God, reveals to us that water baptism is our *public initiation* and *official reception* into the church of Jesus Christ. So, even though God accepts us when we believe, we must also be accepted (or received) by our new family, the Body of Christ. This is because we are not called to isolation, but community. It is through our baptism in water that we publicly declare our faith and are *formally* accepted by the Body of Christ as a member of the Church, the family of God.

Another way to look at it, is that we are often told that we have passed an exam before we receive an *official* certificate or are told that we have been given a job before we receive the *official* paperwork. The *public ceremony / formal certification* is significant for one's existence within the wider community/public;

however, the initial authorisation / acceptance is always given privately before these takes place.

Similarly, when we accept Jesus' proposal at salvation, a new level of commitment is entered, an agreement is made in our heart; Jesus becomes the Lord of our life, He becomes one spirit with our spirit, accepts us and gives us a place in His Body. In our heart we know this, and Jesus knows; however, water baptism is the *outward sign* that publicly signifies that we have received a position into His Body; it is the *formal* recognition that we are part of His church.

> *And baptism, which is a figure [of their deliverance], does now also save you [from inward questionings and fears], not by the removing of outward body filth [bathing], but by [providing you with] the answer of a good and clear conscience (inward cleanness and peace) before God [because you are demonstrating what you believe to be yours] through the resurrection of Jesus Christ.*
> *(1 Peter 3:21, AMPC)*

So you see, baptism doesn't save us (we are saved by grace through faith); however, for the *believer*, it is an answer to God from a clean conscience because *you know* you have been saved by faith. This is why, in the Bible, we often see people getting baptised almost immediately after receiving the Good News— they are responding from a clear conscience purified by faith (Acts 15:9).

> *Those who believed what Peter said were baptized and added to the church that day—about 3,000 in all. (Acts 2:41, NLT)*

> *And Crispus, the chief ruler of the synagogue, believed on the Lord with all his house; and many of the Corinthians hearing believed, and were baptized. (Acts 18:8)*

Without faith, baptism has no significance; it is only powerful because of Christ and His resurrection. If a person does not believe that Jesus died for their sin and that God raised Him from the dead as Lord, then water baptism has no more spiritual significance than a bath.

> *He that <u>believeth</u> and is baptized shall be saved; but he that <u>believeth not</u> shall be damned. (Mark 16:16, emphasis mine)*

> *And as they went on their way, they came unto a certain water: and the eunuch said,*

> *See, here is water; what doth hinder me to be baptized? And Philip said, <u>If thou believest with all thine heart, thou mayest</u>. And he answered and said, I believe that Jesus Christ is the Son of God. (Acts 8:36-27, emphasis mine)*

> *But <u>when they believed the good news</u> (the Gospel) about the kingdom of God and the name of Jesus Christ (the Messiah) as Philip preached it, <u>they were baptized, both men and women</u>. (Acts 8:12, AMPC, emphasis mine)*

Baptism is powerful because through it a believer (by faith) dies to this world and raises to new life in Christ.

> *For you were buried with Christ when you were baptized. And with him you were raised to new life because you trusted the mighty power of God, who raised Christ from the dead. (Colossians 2:12, NLT)*

> *Or have you forgotten that when we were joined with Christ Jesus in baptism, we joined him in his death? For we died and were buried with Christ by baptism. And just as Christ was raised from the dead by the glorious power of the Father, now we also may live new lives.*

> *Since we have been united with him in his death, we will also be raised to life as he was. (Romans 6:3-5, NLT)*

Biblical baptism is a burial of the flesh (old man) and therefore, baptism is a full immersion into water, not a sprinkling.

> *He ordered the carriage to stop, and <u>they went down into the water</u>, and Philip baptized him. When they came <u>up out of the water</u>, the Spirit of the Lord snatched Philip away. The eunuch never saw him again but went on his way rejoicing. (Acts 8:38-39, NLT, emphasis mine)*

When Jesus was on the earth, He was baptised showing us the way. If He saw baptism as a necessity to fulfil all righteousness, why should we see it any other way?

> *Then cometh Jesus from Galilee to Jordan unto John, to be baptized of him. But John forbad him, saying, I have need to be baptized of thee, and comest thou to me? And Jesus answering said unto him, Suffer it to be so now: for thus it becometh us to fulfil all righteousness. Then he suffered him. (Matthew 3:13-15)*

It was because of what happened at Jesus' water baptism that John the Baptist was able to identify Him as the Messiah. If John or Jesus had failed to "fulfil all righteousness" by refusing to obey God's command of baptism, John would not have been able to testify of Jesus. Similarly, it is through our obedience in water baptism, that those in Christ before us, are able to publicly testify that we are members of His Body.

> *And I knew him not: but he that sent me to baptize with water, the same said unto me, Upon whom thou shalt see the Spirit descending, and remaining on him, the same is he which baptizeth with the Holy Ghost. (John 1:33)*

Baptism is a biblical ordinance that all believers are to partake in. Just before Jesus ascended back to Heaven, He gave His disciples a command to *teach* all nations and to *baptise* those who believe. This commandment has been coined the "Great Commission" and is the responsibility of every member of the Body of Christ. As believers, we all have the responsibility to teach all nations to obey Jesus (in the sphere the Lord has called us to) and that includes baptism. If we are going to lead by example, then we ourselves need to obey Jesus and be baptised.

> *Go then and make disciples of all the nations, baptizing them into the name of the Father and of the Son and of the Holy Spirit, Teaching them to observe everything that I have commanded you, and behold, I am with you all the days (perpetually, uniformly, and on every occasion), to the [very] close and consummation of the age. Amen (so let it be). (Matthew 28:19-20, AMPC)*

CHAPTER 5:

BAPTISM WITH THE HOLY GHOST

At the point of salvation, the veil that separated us from God is removed (2 Corinthians 3:16) and our spirit becomes one with His spirit (1 Corinthians 6:17). We are translated from darkness and placed into His Kingdom of Light; we are placed into His Body, His Church. We are no longer spiritually dead, but now alive through Christ. Through our water baptism, we join in Christ's death and publicly demonstrate our faith in His resurrection; we are no longer slaves to sin, we are new creations, pure and holy unto God.

> *Therefore if any man be in Christ, he is a new creature: old things are passed away; behold, all things are become new.*
> *(2 Corinthians 5:17)*

Many believers are content to stop here... but there is more. After Jesus resurrected, He told His disciples to wait for the promise of the Father— *the Holy Ghost*.

> *For John truly baptized with water; but ye shall be baptized with the Holy Ghost not many days hence. (Acts 1:5)*

> *But ye shall receive power, after that the Holy Ghost is come upon you: and ye shall be witnesses unto me both in Jerusalem, and in all Judaea, and in Samaria, and unto the uttermost part of the earth. (Acts 1:8)*

Water baptism is for the forgiveness of sins i.e. salvation; however, baptism with the Holy Ghost is for *power!* Both water baptism and baptism with the Holy Ghost are an *outward sign* of faith; however, water baptism is conducted by other members of the Body of Christ, whilst Jesus is the One that baptises with the Holy Ghost.

> *John answered, saying unto them all, I indeed baptize you with water; but one mightier than I cometh, the latchet of whose shoes I am not worthy to unloose: he shall baptize you with the Holy Ghost and with fire: (Luke 3:16)*

> *I indeed have baptized you with water: but he shall baptize you with the Holy Ghost. (Mark 1:8)*

Baptism in water is an outward sign of *your decision* to follow Jesus, whilst baptism with the

Holy Ghost is an outward sign of *Jesus' decision* to choose you! Essentially, water baptism is our public response to Jesus, whilst baptism with the Holy Ghost is Jesus' public response to us.

WHAT IS THE HOLY GHOST BAPTISM?

As initially mentioned, baptism is a word that means immersed or submerged. To be baptised with the Holy Ghost is to be immersed or submerged by the third member of the Godhead, the Holy Ghost (also called the Holy Spirit in some Bible translations). He is the One that is on the earth with us today. He was the One Who convicted us of sin and was the One Who enabled us to declare that Jesus Christ is Lord.

> *And when he comes, he will convict the world of its sin, and of God's righteousness, and of the coming judgment. (John 16:8, NLT)*

> *Wherefore I give you to understand, that no man speaking by the Spirit of God calleth Jesus accursed: and that no man can say that Jesus is the Lord, but by the Holy Ghost. (1 Corinthians 12:3)*

The Holy Ghost is the Spirit of Truth, our Comforter and our Teacher. He doesn't speak of His own accord, but only what He hears from the Father and the Son.

> *When the Spirit of truth comes, he will guide you into all truth. He will not speak on his own but will tell you what he has heard. He will tell you about the future. (John 16:13, NLT)*

> *Even the Spirit of truth; whom the world cannot receive, because it seeth him not, neither knoweth him: but ye know him; for he dwelleth with you, and shall be in you. (John 14:17)*

> *But the Comforter, which is the Holy Ghost, whom the Father will send in my name, he shall teach you all things, and bring all things to your remembrance, whatsoever I have said unto you. (John 14:26)*

At the point of salvation, we are baptised into the spiritual Body of Christ, i.e. *our spirit* experiences baptism. However, when we are baptised (submerged) with the Holy Ghost we experience an infilling / flooding *of the heart*, i.e. *our soul* experiences a baptism—an overflow of love. This is the power that Jesus was talking about, this is the power that enables us to be a witness.

> *And this hope will not lead to disappointment. For we know how dearly God loves us, because he has given us the Holy Spirit to fill our hearts with his love. (Romans 5:5, NLT)*

We are each a three part being—we are a spirit, with a soul (mind, will and emotions), living in a body. As we discussed in chapter 3, our spirit becomes one with Jesus' Spirit at salvation. So, though we *have* the Holy Ghost at salvation, we are yet to *receive* Him into our heart (soul). When Jesus baptises us with the Holy Ghost, the Holy Ghost fills our hearts with the love of God. Prior to this infilling, although we are saved, we do not yet receive His power; we are not yet able to operate effectively as witnesses of Christ. At salvation, we have access to everything Jesus offers; however, when we are baptised with the Holy Ghost, we truly begin to receive of the gift.

> *Anyone who believes in me may come and drink! For the Scriptures declare, 'Rivers of living water will flow from his heart.'" (When he said "living water," he was speaking of the Spirit, who would be given to everyone believing in him. But the Spirit had not yet*

> *been given, because Jesus had not yet entered into his glory.) (John 7:38-39, AMPC)*

In a nutshell, the baptism with the Holy Ghost is where our hearts are filled with the love of God to an *overflow* for the first time; it is where rivers of living water begin to flow from our belly (heart). It is this love that casts out all fear and enables us to boldly go out and do what God has called us to do.

> *There is no fear in love [dread does not exist], but full-grown (complete, perfect) love turns fear out of doors and expels every trace of terror! For fear brings with it the thought of punishment, and [so] he who is afraid has not reached the full maturity of love [is not yet grown into love's complete perfection].*
> *(1 John 4:18, AMPC)*

> *And when they had prayed, the place was shaken where they were assembled together; and they were all filled with the Holy Ghost, and they spake the word of God with boldness. (Acts 4:31)*

Being *full* of the Holy Ghost (present tense) is supposed to be the lifestyle of a believer; this is the Lord's desire for us as we grow in spiritual maturity—to be consistently full of the love of God. Unfortunately, many within the Body of Christ are content to be filled (past tense) only the first time.

> *And Jesus being <u>full of the Holy Ghost</u> returned from Jordan, and was led by the Spirit into the wilderness, (Luke 4:1, emphasis mine)*

HOW CAN I KNOW IF I'VE BEEN BAPTISED WITH THE HOLY GHOST?

The book of Acts, in the New Testament, records the events of the early church. As we read through this book, we are able to see a number of instances in which believers were baptised with the Holy Ghost. At times this took place before they were baptised in water, and at other times it was after. Regardless, of which way around these took place, by looking through the examples in scripture, we are able to identify the signs that let you know you have been baptised with the Holy Ghost.

- THE DAY OF PENTECOST

Fifty days after Jesus ascended back to Heaven, the Holy Ghost was poured out upon the first believers. 120 believers (both men and women) had been in an upper room waiting to be baptised with the Holy Ghost and receive power to witness, just as Jesus had said. Here's what happened:

> *And when the day of Pentecost was fully come, they were all with one accord in one place. And suddenly there came a sound from heaven as of a rushing mighty wind, and it filled all the house where they were sitting. And there appeared unto them cloven tongues like as of fire, and it sat upon each of them. And they were all filled with the Holy Ghost, and began to speak with other tongues, as the Spirit gave them utterance. (Acts 2:1-4)*

This is the first recording of believers being baptised with the Holy Ghost. Here we see a few things take place that are observable to the human senses:

1. There was a sound from heaven like a rushing mighty wind

2. Tongues of fire appeared and sat on each of them
3. They spoke with other tongues (unlearned languages) by the Spirit's ability, declaring the wonderful works of God (see Acts 2:11).

Wow!

Now, before we can deduce that this will be what the baptism with the Holy Ghost will look like for everyone, let's look at a few more examples to see what remains the same, and what is unique to the specific work God is doing in each instance.

- THE PEOPLE OF SAMARIA

The Samaritans were a group of people who were half Jew and half Gentile. Acts 8 records when the people of Samaria were baptised with the Holy Ghost.

But when they believed Philip preaching the things concerning the kingdom of God, and the name of Jesus Christ, they were baptized, both men and women. Then Simon himself believed also: and when he was baptized, he continued with Philip, and wondered, beholding the miracles and signs which were done. Now when the apostles which were at Jerusalem heard that Samaria had received the word of God, they sent unto them Peter and John: Who, when they were come down, prayed for them, that they might receive the Holy Ghost: (For as yet he was fallen upon none of them: only they were baptized in the name of the Lord Jesus.) Then laid they their hands on them, and they received the Holy Ghost. And when Simon saw that through laying on of the apostles' hands the Holy Ghost was given, he offered them money, Saying, Give me also this power, that on whomsoever I lay hands, he may receive the Holy Ghost. But Peter said unto him, Thy money perish with thee, because thou hast thought that the gift of God may be purchased with money. (Acts 8:12-20)

In this instance, the Samaritans had already received the word and had been baptised in water. It was only when the apostles, Peter & John, came and laid hands on them that the people were baptised with the Holy Ghost. We are not told exactly what observable signs there were for these people; however, the fact that it says "Simon saw" indicates, that he was able to observe some sign/s that let him know something supernatural had taken place.

- THE FIRST GENTILES

Let's now go to Acts 10, where we see the first Gentiles being baptised with the Holy Ghost.

> *While Peter yet spake these words, the Holy Ghost fell on all them which heard the word. And they of the circumcision which believed were astonished, as many as came with Peter, because that on the Gentiles also was poured out the gift of the Holy Ghost. For they heard them speak with tongues, and magnify God. Then answered Peter, Can any man forbid water, that these should not be baptized, which have received the Holy Ghost as well as we? And he commanded them to be baptized in the name of the Lord. Then prayed they him to tarry certain days.*
> *(Acts 10:44-48)*

In this instance there was no rushing mighty wind and no tongues of fire. However, this passage does mention that the Jews were able to recognise what had taken place because the Gentiles spoke with tongues and magnified God.

- THE DISCIPLES AT EPHESUS

Acts 19, records another incident where a group of disciples were baptised with the Holy Ghost.

> *While Apollos was in Corinth, Paul traveled through the interior regions until he reached Ephesus, on the coast, where he found several believers. "Did you receive the Holy Spirit when you believed?" he asked them. "No," they replied, "we haven't even heard that there is a Holy Spirit." "Then what baptism did you experience?" he asked. And they replied, "The baptism of John." Paul said, "John's baptism called for repentance from sin. But John himself told the people to believe in the one who would come later, meaning Jesus." As soon as they heard this, they were baptized in the name of the Lord Jesus. Then when Paul laid his hands on them, the Holy Spirit came on them, and they spoke in other tongues and prophesied. There were about twelve men in all. (Acts 19:1-7, NLT)*

The Bible is very clear whether a person is a disciple (believer) or not. When introducing a person, if the scripture mentions that a person is a believer / disciple then it means they are saved. If it simply calls them a man or woman, then they are yet to be saved.

In this passage, the men that Paul meets are introduced as believers. However, because they had received John's baptism and not the baptism of Jesus Christ, they did not know about the Holy Ghost that was promised. Remember from the message Peter preached, the baptism with the Holy Ghost was a fundamental truth along with repentance, faith and baptism in water:

> *Peter replied, "Each of you must repent of your sins and turn to God, and be baptized in the name of Jesus Christ for the forgiveness of your sins. Then you will receive the gift of the Holy Spirit. (Acts 2:38, NLT)*

These men at Ephesus were disciples, but they had not yet been baptised with the Holy Ghost. After Paul revealed the fundamentals of what they were supposed to receive through Christ, these men were baptised in the name of Jesus and received the Holy Ghost. In this instance, the observable signs were that they spoke in tongues and prophesied.

Having looked through all the examples in the book of Acts, we see that there is always something observable that takes place when a believer is baptised with the Holy Ghost. In the three examples that specifically mention what those signs were, the common theme was a *verbal sign,* i.e. they spoke in tongues and prophesied / magnified God.

> *...for out of the abundance (overflow) of the heart his mouth speaks. (Luke 6:45b, AMPC)*

Thinking back to what we spoke about regarding the Holy Ghost baptism being an infilling and flooding of the heart, it makes sense then that a supernatural *verbal* sign would accompany baptism with the Holy Ghost. Both speaking in tongues and prophecy are huge topics on their own, but below is a simple definition to help you identify them at a basic level:

- SPEAKING IN TONGUES

Speaking in a language that you have not learned. You may or may not understand what you are saying; however, if you do understand, it would be because the Spirit is giving you a supernatural ability to interpret your tongue. It is also possible that if there are people around you, somebody may be able to understand what you are saying (due to it being their native language or the fact that the Spirit is giving them the ability to interpret), (see 1 Corinthians 14:1-33 & Acts 2:1-11).

- PROPHESYING

The divine inspiration to speak out the present and future heart, thoughts and plans of God; speaking that which could not be known but by the Spirit of God. To prophesy is to testify of Jesus (truth) leading to edification, exhortation and comfort for the hearer (see Revelation 19:10, 1 Corinthians 14:1-33 & 1 Corinthians 12:10).

- MAGNIFYING GOD

Speaking out about how great God is, exalting Him in a bold way that is uncanny to your personality. It is possible to magnify God through tongues (unlearned languages) as well as in your native language.

If you experience an infilling (flooding of love that feels like a rushing river) and you begin to feel an overwhelming desire to speak in tongues and prophesy/magnify God from the overflow of your heart (for the first time), then you are experiencing your baptism with the Holy Ghost.

Yield to His love, and from the overflow of your heart, let your mouth speak!

The baptism with the Holy Ghost is not something reserved for especially "spiritual" people. This is something the Lord has promised all believers and is one of the fundamentals of our faith. Our heavenly Father is a good Father, and if you ask Him for the Holy Ghost, He is sure to give Him to you.

> *"And so I tell you, keep on asking, and you will receive what you ask for. Keep on seeking, and you will find. Keep on knocking, and the door will be opened to you. For everyone who asks, receives. Everyone who seeks, finds. And to everyone who knocks, the door will be opened. "You fathers—if your children ask for a fish, do you give them a snake instead? Or if they ask for an egg, do you give them a scorpion? Of course not! So if you sinful people know how to give good gifts to your children, how much more will your heavenly Father give the Holy Spirit to those who ask him." (Luke 11:9-13, NLT)*

CHAPTER 6:

LAYING ON OF HANDS

The laying on of hands is a practice that we see throughout both the Old and New Testament. The term itself means to place the underside of your hand onto the body of another (most commonly the head) and is accompanied by prayer, blessing or decrees of different kinds. In short, the laying on of hands is a public symbol of *transference* or *endorsement* and is done when praying for another or to formally release them for a special work according to the will of God.

LAYING HANDS TO RECEIVE THE BAPTISM WITH THE HOLY GHOST

Seeing as we have just looked at the baptism with the Holy Ghost, let's begin here when looking at the laying on of hands. As we saw in the previous chapter, the practice of laying hands can be used when praying for people to receive the Holy Ghost.

And when Paul had laid his hands upon them, the Holy Ghost came on them; and they spake with tongues, and prophesied. (Acts 19:6)

Then laid they their hands on them, and they received the Holy Ghost. (Acts 8:17)

We know that it is the Lord Jesus that baptises with the Holy Ghost; therefore, we cannot say that people receive the Holy Ghost because of the laying on of hands. However, just as water baptism is a powerful symbol for salvation, the laying on of hands is a powerful symbol for impartation from the Lord. It is not the hands of the person that contain the power, but it is the Lord Jesus in Whom the person who lays hands (and the person on whom hands are being laid), place their faith.

People may receive the baptism with the Holy Ghost with or without the laying on of hands; however, the laying on of hands is a physical and public practice that ignites faith to receive.

LAYING HANDS TO HEAL

> *And these signs shall follow them that believe; In my name shall they cast out devils; they shall speak with new tongues; They shall take up serpents; and if they drink any deadly thing, it shall not hurt them; they shall lay hands on the sick, and they shall recover. (Mark 16:17-18, emphasis mine)*

Laying hands on the sick and seeing them recover, is something all believers can operate in.

> *As it happened, Publius's father was ill with fever and dysentery. Paul went in and prayed for him, and laying his hands on him, he healed him. (Acts 28:8, NLT)*

Again, it is not our hands that contain the power, but the power stems from Christ in Whom we place our faith—Christ *in us* the hope of glory (Colossians 1:27). By power of attorney, we have the authority to release healing to those in need. We are His Body, and our hands act as a point of contact between the person in need and the Spirit of God, the Healer, in us.

Now when the sun was setting, all they that had any sick with divers diseases brought them unto him; and he laid his hands on every one of them, and healed them.
(Luke 4:40)

Now Jesus was teaching in one of the synagogues on the Sabbath. And there was a woman there who for eighteen years had had an infirmity caused by a spirit (a demon of sickness). She was bent completely forward and utterly unable to straighten herself up or to look upward. And when Jesus saw her, He called [her to Him] and said to her, Woman, you are released from your infirmity! Then He laid [His] hands on her, and instantly she was made straight, and she recognized and thanked and praised God.
(Acts 13:10-13, AMPC)

In the scriptures above, we see that Jesus also laid hands when healing the sick. There is something about actually touching those who are sick and in need of healing that represents the love and compassion of God, our faith and God's willingness to heal. Nonetheless, just as Jesus healed through the laying on of hands, He equally healed without laying hands.

Inside the city, near the Sheep Gate, was the pool of Bethesda, with five covered porches. Crowds of sick people—blind, lame, or paralyzed—lay on the porches. One of the men lying there had been sick for thirty-eight years. When Jesus saw him and knew he had been ill for a long time, he asked him, "Would you like to get well?" "I can't, sir," the sick man said, "for I have no one to put me into the pool when the water bubbles up. Someone else always gets there ahead of me." Jesus told him, "Stand up, pick up your mat, and walk!" Instantly, the man was healed! He rolled up his sleeping mat and began walking! But this miracle happened on the Sabbath,
(John 5:2-9, NLT)

In this scripture above, Jesus healed without touching the man. This again emphasises that the laying on of hands *is not a formula*, but a powerful biblical practice that ignites faith and symbolises the very hand / touch of God.

LAYING HANDS TO BLESS

Laying hands to release a blessing is a concept we see even throughout the Old Testament.

Joseph moved the boys, who were at their grandfather's knees, and he bowed with his face to the ground. Then he positioned the boys in front of Jacob. With his right hand he directed Ephraim toward Jacob's left hand, and with his left hand he put Manasseh at Jacob's right hand. But Jacob crossed his arms as he reached out to lay his hands on the boys' heads. He put his right hand on the head of Ephraim, though he was the younger boy, and his left hand on the head of Manasseh, though he was the firstborn. Then he blessed Joseph and said, "May the God before whom my grandfather Abraham and my father, Isaac, walked—the God who has been my shepherd all my life, to this very day, the Angel who has redeemed me from all harm— may he bless these boys. May they preserve my name and the names of Abraham and Isaac. And may their descendants multiply greatly throughout the earth."

But Joseph was upset when he saw that his father placed his right hand on Ephraim's head. So Joseph lifted it to move it from Ephraim's head to Manasseh's head. "No, my father," he said. "This one is the firstborn. Put your right hand on his head." But his father refused. "I know, my son; I know," he replied. "Manasseh will also become a great people,

> *but his younger brother will become even greater. And his descendants will become a multitude of nations." So Jacob blessed the boys that day with this blessing: "The people of Israel will use your names when they give a blessing. They will say, 'May God make you as prosperous as Ephraim and Manasseh.'" In this way, Jacob put Ephraim ahead of Manasseh. (Genesis 48:12-20, NLT)*

In this passage above, we see Jacob laying his hands on his grandsons to bless them. It was custom that the right hand would be placed upon the eldest when blessing as this signified a place of honour and authority; however, we see that Jacob crossed his hands to signify that the younger would be greater than the older.

Throughout the Old Testament, we see that the Patriarchs blessings over their sons were more than just words, but more so a decree / prophecy into their lives. The laying on of hands were again used as a symbol of authority, impartation and approval.

> *And he took them up in his arms, put his hands upon them, and blessed them. (Mark 10:16)*

One day some parents brought their children to Jesus so he could lay his hands on them and pray for them. But the disciples scolded the parents for bothering him. But Jesus said, "Let the children come to me. Don't stop them! For the Kingdom of Heaven belongs to those who are like these children." And he placed his hands on their heads and blessed them before he left. (Matthew 19:13-15, NLT)

In the scriptures above, we see that Jesus laid both His hands on the children when blessing them. In doing so, He demonstrated God's love and approval of them where others saw them as unworthy.

LAYING HANDS TO RELEASE INTO MINISTRY

The laying on of hands when releasing individuals into ministry, is a public biblical practice that is seen throughout both the Old and New Testament of the Bible. It is again a symbol of God's authority and approval being released to an individual for the work He is calling them to.

The Lord said to Moses, Take Joshua son of Nun, a man in whom is the Spirit, and lay your

hand upon him; And set him before Eleazar the priest and all the congregation and give him a charge in their sight. And put some of your honor and authority upon him, that all the congregation of the Israelites may obey him. He shall stand before Eleazar the priest, who shall inquire for him before the Lord by the judgment of the Urim [one of two articles in the priest's breastplate worn when asking counsel of the Lord for the people]. At Joshua's word the people shall go out and come in, both he and all the Israelite congregation with him. And Moses did as the Lord commanded him. He took Joshua and set him before Eleazar the priest and all the congregation, And he laid his hands upon him and commissioned him, as the Lord commanded through Moses.
(Numbers 27:18-23, AMPC)

Here we see the Lord commanding Moses (a God established leader) to release Joshua as a leader, according to the will of God. The laying on of hands here was public recognition of the fact that God had chosen, appointed and approved Joshua.

We see the laying on of hands used in a similar way in the New Testament as well.

As they ministered to the Lord, and fasted, the Holy Ghost said, Separate me Barnabas and Saul for the work whereunto I have called them. And when they had fasted and prayed, and laid their hands on them, they sent them away. (Acts 13:2-3)

In both examples above, the laying on of hands were used to ordain those whom the Lord had specifically chosen for His work, signifying His authority and His approval. Nevertheless, the laying on of hands can also be used to show delegated authority and public approval from man as we see below.

But as the believers rapidly multiplied, there were rumblings of discontent. The Greek-speaking believers complained about the Hebrew-speaking believers, saying that their widows were being discriminated against in the daily distribution of food. So the Twelve called a meeting of all the believers. They said, "We apostles should spend our time teaching the word of God, not running a food program. And so, brothers, select seven men who are well respected and are full of the Spirit and wisdom. We will give them this responsibility. Then we apostles can spend our time in prayer and teaching the word." Everyone liked this idea, and they chose the

> *following: Stephen (a man full of faith and the*
> *Holy Spirit), Philip, Procorus, Nicanor, Timon,*
> *Parmenas, and Nicolas of Antioch (an earlier*
> *convert to the Jewish faith). These seven were*
> *presented to the apostles, who prayed for*
> *them as they laid their hands on them.*
> *(Acts 6:1-6, NLT)*

In this instance, the command did not come directly from the Lord; however, the apostles had God-given authority to delegate, so did just that. The laying on of hands represented an impartation or delegation of authority to run the food distribution programme and the apostle's public approval for the seven to do so.

LAYING HANDS TOO HASTILY

As we have seen, the laying on of hands signifies public approval and a delegation of authority for ministry. It is a biblical practice (seen in both the Old and New Testament) that has powerful connotations; therefore, the Bible also warns against laying hands too quickly.

> *Do not be in a hurry in the laying on of hands*
> *[giving the sanction of the church too hastily*
> *in reinstating expelled offenders or in*

ordination in questionable cases], nor share or participate in another man's sins; keep yourself pure. (1 Timothy 5:22, AMPC)

The laying on of hands when releasing individuals into ministry is something that needs prayerful consideration and the leading of the Holy Ghost, as appointing individuals into leadership too soon, or wrongfully, can have a detrimental effect on those under their leadership.

LAYING HANDS TO BESTOW GIFTS

As well as to release individuals for ministry, the laying on of hands can also be used to impart spiritual gifts.

Do not neglect the spiritual gift you received through the prophecy spoken over you when the elders of the church laid their hands on you. (1 Timothy 4:14, NLT)

This is why I remind you to fan into flames the spiritual gift God gave you when I laid my hands on you. (2 Timothy 1:6, NLT)

Again, it is important to remember that it is not the individual laying hands that gives the spiritual gifts, it is God.

CHAPTER 7:

RESURRECTION OF THE DEAD

The term *resurrection* is one that means to rise again to life having previously died. Throughout scripture we see a number of examples of people being raised from the dead such as the widow's son in 1 Kings 17:17-24, Lazarus in John 11 and Jairus' daughter in Mark 5:21-43. All these were displays of the compassion and miraculous power of God; however, none compare to the significance of the resurrection of the Lord Jesus Christ.

> *Because if you acknowledge and confess with your lips that Jesus is Lord and in your heart believe (adhere to, trust in, and rely on the truth) that God raised Him from the dead, you will be saved. (Romans 10:9, AMPC)*

> *Praised (honored, blessed) be the God and Father of our Lord Jesus Christ (the Messiah)! By His boundless mercy we have been born again to an ever-living hope through the resurrection of Jesus Christ from the dead, (1 Peter 1:3, AMPC)*

Through the resurrection of Jesus, we receive salvation and the promise of *eternal life*. In all the other examples of resurrection, though they were resurrected, they all died again at a later date. Nevertheless, Jesus died and rose *once for all time* – never to taste death again!

> *Now if we have died with Christ, we believe that we shall also live with Him, Because we know that Christ (the Anointed One), being once raised from the dead, will never die again; death no longer has power over Him. (Romans 6:8-9, AMPC)*

The resurrection of the dead, made available through Jesus, speaks of a resurrection to *eternal life.* Not only do we have the hope of our body raising from the dead (to new life), but we also have the hope that even in death our soul will never die i.e. never be separated from God.

> *Jesus told her, "Your brother will rise again." "Yes," Martha said, "he will rise when everyone else rises, at the last day." Jesus told her, "I am the resurrection and the life. Anyone who believes in me will live, even after dying. Everyone who lives in me and believes in me will never ever die. Do you believe this, Martha?" "Yes, Lord," she told him. "I have*

> *always believed you are the Messiah, the Son of God, the one who has come into the world from God." (John 11:23-27, NLT)*

In the above scripture, Jesus reveals to Mary that her brother Lazarus (who was dead at the time) would live again. Mary initially thought that Jesus was alluding to the Last Day (which we will discuss shortly); however, Jesus was revealing a truth which was unknown until that point—that *He is the resurrection and the life.* For those of us who believe in Him, even if we die *physically,* we never truly die because we have He Who is life itself.

> *And this is the way to have eternal life—to know you, the only true God, and Jesus Christ, the one you sent to earth.*
> *(John 17:3, NLT)*

This is why the scriptures use the term "sleeping" to describe believers who have passed from this life. For though their body be dead, they are alive in Christ.

> *Then he said, "Our friend Lazarus has fallen asleep, but now I will go and wake him up." The disciples said, "Lord, if he is sleeping, he will soon get better!" They thought Jesus*

> *meant Lazarus was simply sleeping, but Jesus*
> *meant Lazarus had died. (John 11:11-13, NLT)*

As believers in Christ Jesus, the resurrection of the dead is absolutely foundational to our faith. The following passage of scripture explains why:

> *But tell me this—since we preach that Christ rose from the dead, why are some of you saying there will be no resurrection of the dead? For if there is no resurrection of the dead, then Christ has not been raised either. And if Christ has not been raised, then all our preaching is useless, and your faith is useless. And we apostles would all be lying about God—for we have said that God raised Christ from the grave. But that can't be true if there is no resurrection of the dead. And if there is no resurrection of the dead, then Christ has not been raised. And if Christ has not been raised, then your faith is useless and you are still guilty of your sins. In that case, all who have died believing in Christ are lost! And if our hope in Christ is only for this life, we are more to be pitied than anyone in the world. But in fact, Christ has been raised from the dead. He is the first of a great harvest of all who have died.*

So you see, just as death came into the world through a man, now the resurrection from the dead has begun through another man. Just as everyone dies because we all belong to Adam, everyone who belongs to Christ will be given new life. But there is an order to this resurrection: Christ was raised as the first of the harvest; then all who belong to Christ will be raised when he comes back. After that the end will come, when he will turn the Kingdom over to God the Father, having destroyed every ruler and authority and power. For Christ must reign until he humbles all his enemies beneath his feet. And the last enemy to be destroyed is death. For the Scriptures say, "God has put all things under his authority." (Of course, when it says "all things are under his authority," that does not include God himself, who gave Christ his authority.) Then, when all things are under his authority, the Son will put himself under God's authority, so that God, who gave his Son authority over all things, will be utterly supreme over everything everywhere. (1 Corinthians 15:12-28, NLT)

So you see, it is essential for us to believe that there is a resurrection of the dead, because without this, how can we believe in the resurrection of Christ?

And God will raise us from the dead by his power, just as he raised our Lord from the dead. (1 Corinthians 6:14, NLT)

It is the resurrection of Jesus that makes our own resurrection a reality. Because He is risen, we know that we too will rise when He returns. This is what we will look at next.

THE LAST DAY

And this is the will of him that sent me, that every one which seeth the Son, and believeth on him, may have everlasting life: and I will raise him up at the last day. (John 6:40)

The Last Day is a term used in scripture to refer to the day when the Lord Jesus will return to resurrect those that are His.

And now, dear brothers and sisters, we want you to know what will happen to the believers who have died so you will not grieve like people who have no hope. For since we believe that Jesus died and was raised to life again, we also believe that when Jesus returns, God will bring back with him the believers who have died. We tell you this directly from the Lord: We who are still living when the Lord returns will not meet him ahead of those who have died. For the Lord himself will come down from heaven with a commanding shout, with the voice of the archangel, and with the trumpet call of God. First, the believers who have died will rise from their graves. Then, together with them, we who are still alive and remain on the earth will be caught up in the clouds to meet the Lord in the air. Then we will be with the Lord forever. So encourage each other with these words. (1 Thessalonians 4:13-18, NLT)

As we can see, we will not all die physically; however, those believers who have died (in body) will be resurrected on the Last Day, and we who are still alive will join them to meet the Lord in the air. We will not keep the same mortal body that we have now though. No, we will all receive a new, incorruptible, immortal body.

So also is the resurrection of the dead. It is sown in corruption; it is raised in incorruption: It is sown in dishonour; it is raised in glory: it is sown in weakness; it is raised in power: It is sown a natural body; it is raised a spiritual body. There is a natural body, and there is a spiritual body. (1 Corinthians 15:42-44)

What I am saying, dear brothers and sisters, is that our physical bodies cannot inherit the Kingdom of God. These dying bodies cannot inherit what will last forever. But let me reveal to you a wonderful secret. We will not all die, but we will all be transformed! It will happen in a moment, in the blink of an eye, when the last trumpet is blown. For when the trumpet sounds, those who have died will be raised to live forever. And we who are living will also be transformed. For our dying bodies must be transformed into bodies that will never die; our mortal bodies must be transformed into immortal bodies. (1 Corinthians 15:50-53, NLT)

When Jesus resurrected, He had a body that was able to be seen and touched (John 20:27), that was able to eat (Luke 24:41-43) yet was also able to transport through walls (John 20:26)! This is the type of body that we will also have—one of flesh and bones, but not of flesh and blood.

Now this I say, brethren, that flesh and blood cannot inherit the kingdom of God; neither doth corruption inherit incorruption. (1 Corinthians 15:50)

Behold my hands and my feet, that it is I myself: handle me, and see; for a spirit hath

not flesh and bones, as ye see me have.
(Luke 24:39)

Beloved, now are we the sons of God, and it
doth not yet appear what we shall be: but we
know that, when he shall appear, we shall be
like him; for we shall see him as he is.
(1 John 3:2)

TWO RESURRECTIONS

At the last day, we who are Christ's can look forward to the resurrection of the righteous; however, the Bible mentions two resurrections. The first is the resurrection of the righteous (as we have discussed), whilst the second is the resurrection of the unrighteous.

Having [the same] hope in God which these
themselves hold and look for, that there is to
be a resurrection both of the righteous and
the unrighteous (the just and the unjust). (Acts
24:15, AMPC)

The resurrection of the righteous is quite literally called the First Resurrection. We know that righteousness is a gift through salvation (Romans 5:17) received by faith in Christ alone. To be part of this resurrection is to have your name written in the Lamb's Book of Life and offers you the honour of reigning with Christ during His millennial reign.

> *Then I saw thrones, and the people sitting on them had been given the authority to judge. And I saw the souls of those who had been beheaded for their testimony about Jesus and for proclaiming the word of God. They had not worshiped the beast or his statue, nor accepted his mark on their foreheads or their hands. They all came to life again, and they reigned with Christ for a thousand years. This is the first resurrection. (The rest of the dead did not come back to life until the thousand years had ended.) Blessed and holy are those who share in the first resurrection. For them the second death holds no power, but they will be priests of God and of Christ and will reign with him a thousand years. (Revelation 20:4-6, NLT)*

There is a one-thousand year period between the first resurrection and the second. During this time, satan is bound in the Bottomless Pit, and Jesus reigns on the earth (and we who are His reign with Him).

> *And I saw an angel come down from heaven, having the key of the bottomless pit and a*

> *great chain in his hand. And he laid hold on the dragon, that old serpent, which is the Devil, and Satan, and bound him a thousand years, And cast him into the bottomless pit, and shut him up, and set a seal upon him, that he should deceive the nations no more, till the thousand years should be fulfilled: and after that he must be loosed a little season. (Revelation 20:1-3)*

It is after the millennial reign of Christ on this earth, that the second resurrection will take place. This is the resurrection of the *unjust*, the resurrection of *judgement*. For all who choose not to believe in Jesus, not to put their trust in Him, they choose to reject His salvation and must pay the penalty for their own sin which is death (Romans 6:23).

> *Then they will go away into eternal punishment, but those who are just and upright and in right standing with God into eternal life. (Matthew 25:46, AMPC)*

It is not God's will that anyone would perish, but He has given us all free will to choose. The only way to be made right with God is through Christ. He is our Ark; He is our Salvation. The reason Jesus came is so that we would not have to be judged for our sin. Nevertheless, for all who refuse Him, judgement is the result.

> *"For this is how God loved the world: He gave his one and only Son, so that everyone who believes in him will not perish but have eternal life. God sent his Son into the world not to judge the world, but to save the world through him. There is no judgment against anyone who believes in him. But anyone who does not believe in him has already been judged for not believing in God's one and only Son. And the judgment is based on this fact: God's light came into the world, but people loved the darkness more than the light, for their actions were evil. All who do evil hate the light and refuse to go near it for fear their sins will be exposed. But those who do what is right come to the light so others can see that they are doing what God wants." (John 3:16-21, NLT)*

We will look more at the judgement of the unjust in the next chapter.

CHAPTER 8:

ETERNAL JUDGEMENT

A judgement is a decision, verdict or conclusion. The eternal judgement is therefore the *final* decision, verdict and conclusion of man—one that will not be changed once made—*for all eternity*.

> *And as it is appointed unto men once to die, but after this the judgment: (Hebrews 9:27)*

THE JUDGEMENT OF THE WICKED

Let's begin by looking at the verdict for those that reject Jesus.

> *But by the same word the present heavens and earth have been stored up (reserved) for fire, being kept until the day of judgment and destruction of the ungodly people.*
> *(2 Peter 3:7, AMPC)*

Unfortunately, there is a day of judgement *and destruction* awaiting all those who reject the Son, Jesus Christ. As we saw earlier, it is not God's will for anyone to perish, this is precisely why He sent Jesus. Nevertheless, each of us has a choice. The Father has already given everything, and today He still has the Holy Ghost and the Church, the Body of Christ, functioning in the earth in the hope that men may hear the Good News and repent.

> *The Lord does not delay and is not tardy or slow about what He promises, according to some people's conception of slowness, but He is long-suffering (extraordinarily patient) toward you, not desiring that any should perish, but that all should turn to repentance. (2 Peter 3:9, AMPC)*

The Lord is deliberately patient, giving people as much time as possible. We each have our entire lives to repent and place our faith in Jesus (although no man knows how long their life might be). Nevertheless, there are still some who will refuse to repent and refuse to choose Christ.

> *And the fourth angel poured out his vial upon the sun; and power was given unto him to scorch men with fire. And men were scorched with great heat, and blasphemed the name of God, which hath power over these plagues: <u>and they repented not to give him</u>*

> _glory_. *And the fifth angel poured out his vial upon the seat of the beast; and his kingdom was full of darkness; and they gnawed their tongues for pain, And blasphemed the God of heaven because of their pains and their sores, and repented not of their deeds. (Revelation 16:8-11, emphasis mine)*

When the Lord Jesus returns to judge the ungodly, it will be to bring His wrath and to judge unrighteousness once and for all. In the same way that the Lord destroyed the earth and the wicked with water in the days of Noah, the same way it shall be at the final judgement, but this time with _fire_.

> *Then he used the water to destroy the ancient world with a mighty flood. And by the same word, the present heavens and earth have been stored up for fire. They are being kept for the day of judgment, when ungodly people will be destroyed. ...But the day of the Lord will come as unexpectedly as a thief. Then the heavens will pass away with a terrible noise, and the very elements themselves will disappear in fire, and the earth and everything on it will be found to deserve judgment. (2 Peter 3:6-7, 10, NLT)*

The Day of the Lord is that day when Jesus will judge by fire all those who have rejected His Lordship and saving grace.

> *For he [God] has set a day for judging the world with justice by the man he has appointed, and he proved to everyone who this is by raising him [Jesus] from the dead."* (Acts 17:31, NLT *brackets mine)*

> *Dear friends, if we deliberately continue sinning after we have received knowledge of the truth, there is no longer any sacrifice that will cover these sins. There is only the terrible expectation of God's judgment and the raging fire that will consume his enemies.* (Hebrews 10:26-27, NLT)

The heavens and the earth as we know them will be consumed and destroyed, along with satan, his demons and all those who have rejected Christ Jesus.

> *When the thousand years come to an end, Satan will be let out of his prison. He will go out to deceive the nations—called Gog and Magog—in every corner of the earth. He will gather them together for battle—a mighty army, as numberless as sand along the seashore. And I saw them as they went up on*

the broad plain of the earth and surrounded God's people and the beloved city. But fire from heaven came down on the attacking armies and consumed them. Then the devil, who had deceived them, was thrown into the fiery lake of burning sulfur, joining the beast and the false prophet. There they will be tormented day and night forever and ever. And I saw a great white throne and the one sitting on it. The earth and sky fled from his presence, but they found no place to hide. I saw the dead, both great and small, standing before God's throne. And the books were opened, including the Book of Life. And the dead were judged according to what they had done, as recorded in the books. The sea gave up its dead, and death and the grave gave up their dead. And all were judged according to their deeds. Then death and the grave were thrown into the lake of fire. This lake of fire is the second death. And anyone whose name was not found recorded in the Book of Life was thrown into the lake of fire. (Revelation 20:7-15, NLT)

As we saw previously, the second resurrection takes place after the millennial reign of Christ, whilst the first resurrection takes place before. All those who are part of the second resurrection will be judged according to their deeds, and everyone whose name is not found in the Book of Life will be thrown into the Lake of Fire, which is the second death.

> *Blessed and holy are those who share in the first resurrection. For them the second death holds no power, but they will be priests of God and of Christ and will reign with him a thousand years. (Revelation 20:6, NLT)*

For those who were resurrected before the millennial reign, the second death holds no power. However, for the rest, the second death is a fearsome conclusion to life.

> *And do not be afraid of those who kill the body but cannot kill the soul; but rather be afraid of Him who can destroy both soul and body in hell (Gehenna).*
> *(Matthew 10:28, AMPC)*

The second death (The Lake of Fire) is a place where even death and the grave (realm of the dead) are destroyed. The second death is where not only the body is destroyed, but where one's soul is also destroyed—this is the final verdict for all those who reject Jesus.

And He condemned to ruin and extinction the cities of Sodom and Gomorrah, reducing them to ashes [and thus] set them forth as an example to those who would be ungodly; (2 Peter 2:6, AMPC)

The extinction of Sodom and Gomorrah were examples of the extinction that will eventually fall on the ungodly. The Lake of Fire was never created for mankind; nevertheless, for all those who choose to follow satan, that is their fatal end.

Then shall he say also unto them on the left hand, Depart from me, ye cursed, into everlasting fire, prepared for the devil and his angels: (Matthew 25:41)

Let us now look at the judgement of the believer.

THE JUDGEMENT OF THE BELIEVER

As believers, we are saved from the wrath of God. In Christ we are safe, He is our Ark and our Salvation. We can rest assured in the finished work of the cross and righteousness that is by faith, for no person can escape the fires of the second death through their own works, it is solely through faith in Jesus.

For we who put our faith in Christ, we do not need to fear the Lake of Fire, but we can look forward to a new heaven and a new earth. One without pain, without sin and without corruption.

> *Since everything around us is going to be destroyed like this, what holy and godly lives you should live, looking forward to the day of God and hurrying it along. On that day, he will set the heavens on fire, and the elements will melt away in the flames. But we are looking forward to the new heavens and new earth he has promised, a world filled with God's righteousness. (2 Peter 3:11-13, NLT)*

> *And I saw a new heaven and a new earth: for the first heaven and the first earth were passed away; and there was no more sea. And I John saw the holy city, new Jerusalem, coming down from God out of heaven, prepared as a bride adorned for her husband. And I heard a great voice out of heaven saying, Behold, the tabernacle of God is with men, and he will dwell with them, and they shall be his people, and God himself shall be with them, and be their God. And God shall wipe away all tears from their eyes; and there*

shall be no more death, neither sorrow, nor crying, neither shall there be any more pain: for the former things are passed away. (Revelation 21:1-4)

As saints, we have a promise of a new home, one where Heaven and Earth will live as one; God amongst His people as one big family.

JUDGEMENT FOR REWARDS

Through the gift of salvation, we have the promise of eternal life, a new body and a new home. Nevertheless, the Bible is clear that there is still a judgement that we as believers must face.

For we must all appear before the judgment seat of Christ; that every one may receive the things done in his body, according to that he hath done, whether it be good or bad. (2 Corinthians 5:10)

In this passage of scripture, the apostle Paul is speaking to *believers*. Every believer in Jesus Christ will stand before the Judgement Seat of Christ to give an account. This is not the same type of judgement as unbelievers face (which

FUNDAMENTALS: LAYING A FOUNDATION FOR NEW BELIEVERS

takes place before the Great White Throne, see Revelation 20:11); however, this is a judgement where we are rewarded according to our *obedience* in this life. We will be assessed according to our faithfulness in this life, and the Lord will give us more accordingly. The parable of the talents is a good depiction of what will happen.

> *"Again, the Kingdom of Heaven can be illustrated by the story of a man going on a long trip. He called together his servants and entrusted his money to them while he was gone. He gave five bags of silver to one, two bags of silver to another, and one bag of silver to the last—dividing it in proportion to their abilities. He then left on his trip. "The servant who received the five bags of silver began to invest the money and earned five more. The servant with two bags of silver also went to work and earned two more. But the servant who received the one bag of silver dug a hole in the ground and hid the master's money. "After a long time their master returned from his trip and called them to give an account of how they had used his money. The servant to whom he had entrusted the five bags of silver came forward with five more and said, 'Master, you gave me five bags of silver to invest, and I have earned five more.' "The*

master was full of praise. 'Well done, my good and faithful servant. You have been faithful in handling this small amount, so now I will give you many more responsibilities. Let's celebrate together!' "The servant who had received the two bags of silver came forward and said, 'Master, you gave me two bags of silver to invest, and I have earned two more.' "The master said, 'Well done, my good and faithful servant. You have been faithful in handling this small amount, so now I will give you many more responsibilities. Let's celebrate together!' "Then the servant with the one bag of silver came and said, 'Master, I knew you were a harsh man, harvesting crops you didn't plant and gathering crops you didn't cultivate. I was afraid I would lose your money, so I hid it in the earth. Look, here is your money back.' "But the master replied, 'You wicked and lazy servant! If you knew I harvested crops I didn't plant and gathered crops I didn't cultivate, why didn't you deposit my money in the bank? At least I could have gotten some interest on it.' "Then he ordered, 'Take the money from this servant, and give it to the one with the ten bags of silver. To those who use well what they are given, even more will be given, and they will have an abundance. But from those who do nothing, even what little they have will be taken away. Now throw this useless servant into outer

> *darkness, where there will be weeping and gnashing of teeth.' (Matthew 25:14-30, NLT)*

Through this parable we learn that we will each be judged according to what we have been given. It is not so much a matter of *how much* as it is a matter of *how faithful.* The Lord will judge us each proportionally, which means that two people may have differing levels of responsibility, but still be judged equally as faithful. Nevertheless, the Bible does tell us that those of us in positions of leadership will be judged more harshly.

> *Dear brothers and sisters, not many of you should become teachers in the church, for we who teach will be judged more strictly. (James 3:1, NLT)*
>
> *But someone who does not know, and then does something wrong, will be punished only lightly. When someone has been given much, much will be required in return; and when someone has been entrusted with much, even more will be required.*
> *(Luke 12:48, NLT)*

As we can see, we will all be judged according to what the Lord entrusts to us to begin with. It is the Lord that decides what we are given; however, it is our responsibility to respond to Him faithfully with what we have been given. How we steward what we are given to begin with, makes a way for what we are given responsibility over in the millennial reign and in the world to come.

The crowd was listening to everything Jesus said. And because he was nearing Jerusalem, he told them a story to correct the impression that the Kingdom of God would begin right away. He said, "A nobleman was called away to a distant empire to be crowned king and then return. Before he left, he called together ten of his servants and divided among them ten pounds of silver, saying, 'Invest this for me while I am gone.' But his people hated him and sent a delegation after him to say, 'We do not want him to be our king.' "After he was crowned king, he returned and called in the servants to whom he had given the money. He wanted to find out what their profits were. The first servant reported, 'Master, I invested your money and made ten times the original amount!' "'Well done!' the king exclaimed. 'You are a good servant. You have been faithful with the little I entrusted to you, so you will be governor of ten cities as your reward.' "The next servant reported, 'Master, I invested your money and made five times the original amount.' "'Well done!' the king said. 'You will be governor over five cities.' "But the third servant brought back only the original amount of money and said, 'Master, I hid your money and kept it safe. I was afraid because you are a hard man to deal with, taking what isn't yours and harvesting crops you didn't plant.' "'You wicked servant!' the king roared. 'Your own words condemn you. If you knew that I'm a hard man who takes what isn't mine and harvests crops I didn't plant, why didn't you deposit my money in the bank? At least I could have gotten some interest on it.' "Then, turning to the others standing nearby, the king ordered, 'Take the money from this servant, and give it to the one who has ten pounds.' "'But, master,' they said, 'he already has ten pounds!' "'Yes,' the king replied, 'and to those who use well what they are given, even more will be given. But from those who do nothing, even what little they have will be taken away. And as for these enemies of mine who didn't want me to be their king—bring them in and execute them right here in front of me.'" (Luke 19:11-27, NLT)

In this parable, we see that each of the servants were given an equal amount and with that, each multiplied at different quantities. The Lord was pleased with any form of multiplication (although they were rewarded accordingly); however, again we see that a failure to multiply was condemned. Regardless of the amount we begin with, we cannot afford to be lazy or slothful. The Lord expects us to multiply and sees a failure to do so as wicked.

> *But his master answered him, You wicked and lazy and idle servant! Did you indeed know that I reap where I have not sowed and gather [grain] where I have not winnowed? (Matthew 25:26, AMPC)*

> *And throw the good-for-nothing servant into the outer darkness; there will be weeping and grinding of teeth. (Matthew 25:30, AMPC)*

When Jesus returns, it should be our heart to hear the Lord say, "Well done, my good and faithful servant." In order to hear these words, we must live a life where we are diligent to seek His will for our lives and obey as we are led by His Spirit.

In the parable of the sower (see Matthew 13 & Mark 4), the Lord reveals that there are four types of people, or four ways to receive the word of God: 1) the way side, 2) stony places, 3) thorns and 4) good ground. Though all hear the word, it is only those with a heart of good ground who produce fruit (and even then, there are different quantities of fruitfulness: one-hundred-fold, sixty-fold and thirty-fold). We each have a choice as to which person we will be, and our reward will be given accordingly. If we choose to allow persecution or affliction to offend us (cause us to stumble and fall away from faith in Christ), then the result will be the same verdict as that of the unbeliever.

> *[Therefore beware] brethren, take care, lest there be in any one of you a wicked, unbelieving heart [which refuses to cleave to, trust in, and rely on Him], leading you to turn away and desert or stand aloof from the living God. (Hebrews 3:12, AMPC)*

> *And if thy right eye* <u>*offend thee*</u>*, pluck it out, and cast it from thee: for it is profitable for thee that one of thy members should perish, and not that thy whole body should be cast into hell. (Matthew 5:29, emphasis mine)*

Alternatively, if we allow the cares of this world, the deceitfulness of riches and the lusts of other things to choke / hinder us in this life, we will still be saved; nevertheless, we will become *unfruitful* and that which we do have will be taken away from us and given to another more faithful. i.e. we will lose our reward.

But on the judgment day, fire will reveal what kind of work each builder has done. The fire will show if a person's work has any value. If the work survives, that builder will receive a reward. But if the work is burned up, the builder will suffer great loss. The builder will be saved, but like someone barely escaping through a wall of flames. (1 Corinthians 3:13-14, NLT)

Watch out that you do not lose what we have worked so hard to achieve. Be diligent so that you receive your full reward. (2 John 1:8, NLT)

The Lord knows the hearts of us all. We may be able to put on a façade for others to convince them that we are loving and faithful when we are not, or even that we believe when we do not. Nevertheless, all shall be revealed in the end.

So don't make judgments about anyone ahead of time—before the Lord returns. For he will bring our darkest secrets to light and will reveal our private motives. Then God will give to each one whatever praise is due. (1 Corinthians 4:5, NLT)

So, as you close this book and continue to run your race #ForAnEternalPrize, remember this foundational truth: *Jesus is coming back*, and for the believer who remains faithful till the end, *there is a reward to be received*. Selah.

> *And he saith unto me, Seal not the sayings of the prophecy of this book: for the time is at hand. He that is unjust, let him be unjust still: and he which is filthy, let him be filthy still: and he that is righteous, let him be righteous still: and he that is holy, let him be holy still. And, behold, I come quickly; and my reward is with me, to give every man according as his work shall be. I am Alpha and Omega, the beginning and the end, the first and the last. (Revelation 22:10-13)*

NOTES

NOTES

NOTES

RECOMMENDATIONS

For more biblical teaching and resources, visit:

www.believersontrack.com

YouTube: Believers on Track

Instagram: @believersontrack

• •

To connect or find out more about the author, visit:

www.toremathompson.uk

YouTube: Torema Thompson

Instagram: @ToremaThompson